Introduction

The programmes

This production of *Macbeth* is a specially commissioned television version featured within **Middle English**, a series for 11 – 14 year olds which offers a range of resource material to support the teaching of English.

Transmitted in five Parts, **Macbeth** moves swiftly and is marked by high dramatic tension. It is bold yet conventional, faithful to the original, yet eminently accessible. It provides a fresh and clear angle on the play, while the main characters are strongly and richly developed, provoking thought about their motives and insight into their personalities.

The Study Guide

The activities that follow are designed to support viewing the production Part by Part, although several of the activities can be carried out alongside a continuous viewing and reading. It is also assumed that pupils will have access to the full script.

Each section is divided into plot, character and language study, but the emphasis in each varies. Much of the work involves pair or group discussion, but all of it is adaptable. Drama work is included to encourage an active approach to Shakespeare's verse. There is also a focus on pupils developing their own critical responses to both the script and screen versions, while being led to a comparative consideration of the two.

Pupils can work their way through the activities in the order in which they are presented, but flexibility has been built in to allow for a more 'pick-and-mix' approach.

Your feedback is most welcome, so please send any comments about either the production or the Study Guide to:

Adrienne Jones
Education Officer, 4Learning
PO Box 100
Warwick
CV34 6TZ

contents

Macbeth: the Director's view

Macbeth is a story full of 'invisible bullets'. If Duncan is such a good King, why are the Norwegians, the Irish, the Western Isles and two of the strongest clans in Scotland trying to get rid of him?

What deal did Malcolm make with the English in order to secure the loan of 10,000 troops (the equivalent of half a million soldiers today)?

If Malcolm is such an innocent person, how come he is such a liar? What will happen in the future?

It has always taken a butcher to beat a butcher, and the story of Macbeth is no exception. Shakespearean themes are plentiful: the lust for power, the territorial imperative, and imagination versus real politics.

Finally, we are left with an aching sense of a creative spirit dashed on the rock of ambition, and only replaced by cold ruthless pragmatism. Out of the frying pan. Macbeth's crime? To make killing an art. If only he had been able to use that creative force for good.

Do we really want to be ruled by the Malcolms of this world? This is a tale told by an idiot dedicated to English taste. It is the ultimate 'Scottish Play'.

Michael Bogdanov, Director

Macbeth: the Producer's view

I made two major mistakes when I started studying Shakespeare at school.

Firstly, I came to it with the firm belief that he had basically written plays for 'old men in frocks'. And why would that be of interest to any teenager? Secondly, I thought I could do well in my 'O' level exams by learning the text by heart. At one time I could actually quote a whole play from start to finish!

This attitude prevented me from engaging in his plays and from understanding and appreciating his talents as a dramatist. It also prevented me from looking at the action and listening to the words, the beautiful language that he used to make the commonplace interesting and the interesting even more so.

When I read Macbeth, my attitude changed. It opened my eyes to what Shakespeare was all about. I discovered this wonderful story with all the ingredients to appeal to a young audience: fear of the supernatural, the lust for power, envy, blood, murder and mayhem! The same kinds of ingredients you now find in series like Cracker, Prime Suspect and The X Files.

Now, many years later, when setting out to produce this version of Macbeth – or 'The Scottish Play', as it is known – I obviously still wanted the impact of the play to come through the text. But alongside the text it was also important to provide visual stimulation and prompts which would remain in the audience's mind.

There is no sub-plot and the speed of the action heightens the excitement. It was vital that the camera work and editing process should reflect and accentuate this.

Michael Bogdanov, an authoritative and enthusiastic director, was the obvious choice for the project. He was totally sympathetic to the idea of setting the production in an urban industrial landscape, and believed, as I did, that in this kind of post-apocalyptic wilderness we could clearly show a sense of confusion of the usual human order. Scotland is in a state of decay, the communities have become fragmented, and society is frightened of the forces which seem to threaten any remaining sense of order.

Our locations – an abandoned warehouse complex in central Manchester and a disused monastery in Gorton – were perfect for our purposes. By contrast, the English scenes were set against a country house in Cheshire, with well manicured lawns and colourful herbaceous borders.

With the casting of Sean Pertwee and Greta Scacchi as the two central characters, and their strong visual resemblance to each other, I was reminded of a theory of mine from school. It was that Macbeth and his Lady are like two sides of the same coin. Her passionate energies magnify his. She knows him as well as herself, but when she chooses a path that abolishes her femininity, she has nowhere to turn when he rejects her.

Together the two actors provide the means to grasp the emotional reality behind the words. Their concord in evil has great power.

By removing the play from its historical context and making it more filmic, we sought to demonstrate that in its 'timeless' state the central narrative is as strong and exciting as any popular TV drama today, and to encourage a broader interest in Shakespeare's work.

Sue Pritchard, Producer

Macbeth: Quotations

There's no art
To find the mind's construction in the face.

O, full of scorpions is my mind, dear wife!

Will all great Neptune's ocean wash this blood
Clean from my hand?

Yet do I fear thy nature;
It is too full o' the milk of human kindness
To catch the nearest way.

My hands are of your colour; but I shame
To wear a heart so white.

By th'clock, 'tis day,
And yet dark night strangles the travelling lamp.

I am in blood
Stepp'd in so far that, should I wade no more,
Returning were as tedious as go o'er.

Here lay Duncan,
His silver skin laced with his golden blood.

Come, you spirits
That tend on mortal thoughts, unsex me here,
And fill me from the crown to the toe top-full
Of direst cruelty!

Thy bones are marrowless, thy blood is cold;
Thou hast no speculation in those eyes
Which thou dost glare with!

False face must hide what the false hear doth
know.

Thou has it now: king, Cawdor, Glamis, all,
As the weird women promised, and, I fear,
Thou play'dst most foully for't.

I look'd toward Birnam, and anon, methought,
The wood began to move.

All is the fear and nothing is the love.

Tell me, if your art
Can tell so much: shall Banquo's issue ever
Reign in this kingdom?

Receive what cheer you may:
The night is long that never finds the day.

I grant him bloody,
Luxurious, avaricious, false, deceitful,
Sudden, malicious, smacking of every sin
That has a name.

Great Dunsinane he strongly fortifies:
Some say he's mad; others that lesser hate him
Do call it valiant fury.

Stars, hide your fires;
Let not light see my black and deep desires.

Turn, hell-hound, turn!

This disease is beyond my practice.

©1998 Channel Four Learning Limited

Understanding Shakespeare

Before you begin – don't worry!

Tackling a Shakespeare play can often seem daunting. From the moment you begin reading the original script or start watching the television **Macbeth**, you will notice the language. If this is the first Shakespeare play that you have read, you may find the language confusing and difficult. Don't worry: most people find Shakespeare's language confusing at first. You will need to work hard to understand it, but the more effort you put in the more you will get out. *Macbeth* is a play full of action, excitement, violence, tragedy, bravery, treachery, madness, despair and power. The language used may be nearly 375 years old, but it is beautiful, and the emotions and actions of the characters are the same as those of people today. Once you have given some thought and effort to the activities in this booklet you will understand why many people say that Shakespeare was a brilliant writer. Maybe you will see why *Macbeth* is a favourite play of audiences, directors, actors and students alike.

Historical background

Macbeth was first performed when James I was on the throne of England. He was personally terrified of witches. Most people at this time believed that witches were real and possessed horrifying powers. Witches were thought to be able to speak with the devil and use spells and potions to harm their enemies. They could fly through the air, sail in sieves, cause bad weather and storms, wreck ships and kill animals. Witches were blamed for disasters and accidents of all kinds. Women in particular were accused of witchcraft, and when convicted were tortured and executed by being burnt at the stake.

Not only was James afraid of witches, but he had also just survived an attempt to murder him. This murder attempt is now called the Gunpowder Plot. James would have particularly enjoyed watching *Macbeth*. The play would have shown that witches were a very real danger and that those who challenged the King would be punished.

When you have finished reading and working on *Macbeth*, think about what there is in the play that appeals directly to you.

©1998 Channel Four Learning Limited

Macbeth: Part 1

Synopsis

In this Part the main characters are introduced and the atmosphere of the play established. The play opens with three witches planning to meet with Macbeth. As they leave they chant ominous words.

Meanwhile King Duncan is receiving reports of Macbeth's and Banquo's victory. They have bravely put down a rebellion against Duncan. In gratitude, Duncan announces that Macbeth is to be Thane of Cawdor.

The witches mix up a charm to prepare for their meeting with Macbeth. They greet him with the prediction that he will be Thane of Cawdor and King. Banquo is told that his sons will be kings. As the witches vanish, Ross and Angus confirm that Macbeth is now Thane of Cawdor.

Macbeth sees Malcolm as an obstacle to his ambition when Duncan announces that Malcolm is to be his heir.

At Macbeth's castle, Lady Macbeth is reading a letter from her husband. It tells her what has happened. She fears that Macbeth will not be able to fulfill the prophecy, and she begins to plan Duncan's murder.

Duncan arrives at Macbeth's castle and is welcomed by Lady Macbeth with elaborate courtesy. The castle gates clang ominously behind them.

1 The main characters

With a partner, look at the photographs below.

Macbeth

Malcolm

Donalbain

Lady Macbeth

Banquo

a Put a tick by the characters that have appeared so far. Discuss with your partner which one seems to be the most important, which is next most important, and so on.

b Compare your ideas with those of another pair in the class.

c Repeat the activity; this time discuss and agree with your partner about:

◆ who holds the highest social position, who the next highest, and so on.

◆ which is your favourite character so far, which is your next favourite, and so on.

d Choose at least two characters. Write their names into your books. Add detailed comments based on the following:

◆ approximate age

◆ social status (powerful, weak...)

◆ job (if any, or if known)

◆ religious beliefs

◆ appearance (clothes, facial expression, typical gestures...)

◆ speech (hard or easy to understand, direct and clear or flowery, full of imagery, anecdotes, repetitions, rhythmical, like poetry, or chatty, conversational...)

2 The witches

a Look at these pictures of the different presentations of the witches.

The witches play a crucial role in *Macbeth*. Shakespeare chose to open the play with a witches scene. The atmosphere created by the opening scene is very important. Directors of this play have to decide how to present the witches to the best dramatic effect.

◆ Which of the pictures do you find most dramatically pleasing?

◆ Would your choice be better on the stage, on television, or as a film production?

b Imagine that you have been asked to direct the opening scene of *Macbeth*. Make notes and sketches of your ideas. These could include set and costume design. How would you choose to present the witches? As Banquo first describes them,

What are these
So wither'd and so wild in their attire,
That look not like the inhabitants o' the earth,
And yet are on't?

(Act I Scene 3 Lines 39 – 42)

or as something more modern?

◆ Think carefully about how to make the scene interesting and exciting.

◆ How would you want your audience to feel as they watched this scene?

c Design a witches information pamphlet for use during the reign of James I. You need to warn people about the dangers of witches. You may have to do some research in the library or ask a history teacher for help. Consider the following points:

◆ How witches can be identified.

◆ What magical and fantastic powers they have.

◆ What terrible acts they are supposed to be responsible for.

◆ What the law says to do about them.

Think about the layout of your pamphlet, the use of columns, choice of headlines, inclusion of pictures, use of colour, and so on.

7

3 Lady Macbeth

a With a partner, read Lady Macbeth's speech (Act I Scene 5 Lines 38 – 54):

> *The raven himself is hoarse*
> *That croaks the fatal entrance of Duncan*
> *Under my battlements. Come, you spirits*
> *That tend on mortal thoughts, unsex me here,*
> *And fill me from the crown to the toe top-full*
> *Of direst cuelty! make thick my blood;*
> *Stop up the access and passage to remorse,*
> *That no compunctious visitings of nature*
> *Shake my fell purpose, nor keep peace between*
> *The effect and it! Come to my woman's breasts,*
> *And take my milk for gall, you murdering ministers,*
> *Wherever in your sightless substances*
> *You wait on nature's mischief! Come, thick night,*
> *And pall thee in the dunnest smoke of hell,*
> *That my keen knife see not the wound it makes,*
> *Nor heaven peep through the blanket of the dark,*
> *To cry 'Hold, hold!'*

b Still in pairs, work out the most effective way of delivering the speech. In **Part 1** Lady Macbeth speaks her lines as if creating a spell. You may like to include some background sound effects to create even more dramatic intensity. Experiment with whispering and then shouting parts of the speech. Try performing your final version. Compare it with those performed by others.

c Look again at the language of the speech. What makes these images so intense and powerful? In your books write an analysis of this speech. Use the following questions to help you:

◆ What is the general effect of these lines?

◆ Why did Shakespeare use a raven rather than another bird?

◆ Why does Lady Macbeth need to call for help from evil spirits?

◆ Gall is bitter poison. How does Lady Macbeth use this for dramatic effect?

◆ How will the 'thick night' help the Macbeths to murder Duncan?

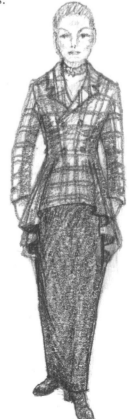

---

4 Quotations

On page 4 are some quotations from the script.

a Read all the quotations, and either cut out and stick down, or copy out, the ones that you recognise from **Part 1**.

b For each quotation, use your version of the play to find out which character says the lines and which act and scene they are from. Write these details neatly next to the quotation, including the exact line reference if possible.

---

5 Points to ponder

Write or discuss:

◆ Which characters so far would you describe as foul and which as fair?

◆ Is Duncan a good King?

◆ What is Banquo thinking at the end of this Part?

◆ Is the Macbeths' marriage a marriage of equals?

◆ How are appearances deceptive?

Macbeth: Part 2

Synopsis

This Part opens with Macbeth struggling with his conscience. He argues that Duncan is a good King and that his murder will provoke vengeance. Ambition is his only motivation to kill. Lady Macbeth persuades him to kill Duncan. She explains her plan to make Duncan's bodyguards drunk, making it easier to kill him.

In the courtyard of Macbeth's castle, Banquo reveals that he has been dreaming of the witches' prophecies. Macbeth, left alone, prepares for Duncan's murder. He imagines he sees a bloody dagger, and his mind is full of evil images.

Macbeth returns to his waiting wife with the bloody daggers. He is now incapable of any further action, and Lady Macbeth has to take them back to the scene of the crime. They are disturbed by knocking at the castle gate, and leave to wash away Duncan's blood.

The drunken porter opens the gate. Macduff goes to waken the King but returns with news of his murder. Macbeth tells the hurriedly assembled group why he killed the bodyguards. Lady Macbeth faints. Malcolm and Donalbain slip away, fearing for their lives.

1 Shall I kill Duncan?

Alone at the beginning of this Part, Macbeth agonises over killing Duncan.

a In small groups, using your copies of the full text, read the uncut version of this speech (Act I Scene 7 Lines 1 – 8):

If it were done when 'tis done, then 'twere well
It were done quickly: if the assassination
Could trammel up the consequence, and catch
With his surcease success; that but this blow
Might be the be-all and the end-all here,
But here, upon this bank and shoal of time,
We'ld jump the life to come. But in these cases
We still have judgement here; that we but teach
Bloody instructions, which, being taught, return
To plague the inventor: this even-handed justice
Commends the ingredients of our poison'd
  chalice
To our own lips. He's here in double trust;
First, as I am his kinsman and his subject,
Strong both against the deed; then, as his host,
Who should against his murderer shut the door,
Not bear the knife myself. Besides, this Duncan
Hath borne his faculties so meek, hath been
So clear in his great office, that his virtues
Will plead like angels, trumpet-tongued, against
The deep damnation of his taking-off;
And pity, like a naked new-born babe,
Striding the blast, or heaven's cherubim, horsed
Upon the sightless couriers of the air,
Shall blow the horrid deed in every eye,
That tears shall drown the wind. I have no spur
To prick the sides of my intent, but only
Vaulting ambition, which o'erleaps itself
And falls on the other.

Some cuts have already been made to the original text. It is important for you to notice the differences between this televised version of the play and the text you are expected to use in examinations.

The cuts that have been made tend to speed up the action of the play. Why might this have been done?

b Compare the uncut version with the transcript printed below, and work out which parts of the text have been cut.

> *If it were done when 'tis done, then 'twere well*
> *It were done quickly. If th'assassination*
> *Could trammel up the consequence and catch*
> *With his surcease, success, that but this blow*
> *Might be the be-all and the end-all – here,*
> *But here, upon this bank and shoal of time,*
> *We'd jump the life to come. But in these cases*
> *We still have judgement here that we but teach*
> *Bloody instructions, which being taught, return*
> *To plague th'inventor.*
> *He's here in double trust:*
> *First, as I am his kinsman and his subject,*
> *Strong both against the deed; then, as his host,*
> *Who should against his murderer shut the door,*
> *Not bear the knife myself.*

c Using the full-length version, work out where the following arguments against the murder appear in Macbeth's soliloquy.

- ◆ Duncan's good qualities as King
- ◆ loyalty
- ◆ vengeance
- ◆ kinship
- ◆ hospitality
- ◆ religious damnation
- ◆ pity
- ◆ horror
- ◆ ambition

2 **What is a man?**

The question of what makes a man runs throughout the play. Each of the characters has their own views as to the qualities that a man should possess.

a With a partner, make a list of ten qualities that you think a man should possess.

b Which of these qualities do you think Macbeth possesses?

c What other qualities are important to include in a description of Macbeth's character?

3 **Is this a dagger which I see before me?**

Familiarise yourself with Macbeth's soliloquy (Act II Scene 1 Lines 33 – 64) as it appears in **Part 2**.

The following section of the text contains many evil images as Macbeth makes his way to murder Duncan.

> *Is this a dagger which I see before me,*
> *The handle toward my hand? Come, let me clutch thee:*
> *I have thee not, and yet I see thee still.*
> *Art thou not, fatal vision, sensible*
> *To feeling as to sight? Or art thou but*
> *A dagger of the mind, a false creation,*
> *Proceeding from the heat-oppressed brain?*
> *I see thee yet, in form as palpable*
> *As this which now I draw.*
> *Thou marshall'st me the way that I was going,*
> *And such an instrument I was to use.*
> *Mine eyes are made the fools o' th'other senses,*
> *Or else worth all the rest. I see thee still.*
> *And on thy blade and dudgeon gouts of blood*
> *Which was not so before. There's no such thing:*
> *It is the bloody business which informs*
> *Thus to mine eyes. Now o'er the one half-world*
> *Nature seems dead, and wicked dreams abuse*
> *The curtained sleep.*
> *Thou sure and firm-set earth,*
> *Hear not my steps, which way they walk, for fear*
> *Thy very stones prate of my whereabout,*
> *And take the present horror from the time,*
> *Which now suits with it. Whiles I threat, he lives;*
> *Words to the heat of deeds too cold breath gives.*
>
> A bell rings.
>
> *I go, and it is done. The bell invites me.*
> *Hear it not, Duncan, for it is a knell*
> *That summons thee to heaven or to hell.*

a Underline any words or phrases that you find particularly striking.

b Most sentences have a subject and a verb. Using two different colours, underline a subject and a verb in each of the sentences of this speech. You might also try looking for other parts of speech such as adjectives. You should find that looking at the text in this way helps you achieve a more detailed understanding of the poetic language used.

c Make a collage representing the images in this speech. Use pictures cut from magazines, key words and phrases from the speech, even sketches you have drawn to symbolise the images.

④ Lord and Lady Macbeth

a Clearly, both Macbeth and Lady Macbeth are disturbed after the murder of Duncan.

◆ Macbeth is unable to say 'Amen'.

◆ He hears a voice saying 'Sleep no more. Macbeth does murder sleep.'

◆ Lady Macbeth has heard strange noises while waiting.

b How will they react to the news that Malcolm and Donalbain have fled?

With a partner discuss how these two characters are feeling at this point in the play.

c Write diary entries for Lord and Lady Macbeth. Diaries are always written in the first person. Remember that these journals are for private thoughts.

You might want to refer to events from the beginning of the play, or concentrate on recent events.

Include:

◆ their feelings about each other

◆ their feelings towards other characters in the play

---

⑤ Quotations

In groups of three or four, look at the quotations on page 4 and find which ones appear in **Part 2**.

a Check the playscript for where they appear and who speaks them.

b Take a quotation each. Learn it by heart, and practise saying it in the group to each other in as many different ways as possible: experiment with different tones of voice, try putting the stress on different words, and so on. When you are satisfied with your way of saying the words, present it to another group or to the whole class.

---

⑥ Points to ponder

Write or discuss:

◆ What is the effect of the Porter scene in the original playscript?

◆ What are Banquo's thoughts in this Part?

◆ When Lady Macbeth faints, is it real or pretended?

◆ Why do Malcolm and Donalbain choose to run away?

◆ Can you predict what will happen next?

13

Macbeth: Part 3

Synopsis

An old man tells Ross of the unnatural happenings in the night. These mirror Duncan's murder. Macduff reports that suspicion for the murder rests on Malcolm and Donalbain. Macbeth has gone to be crowned as King of Scotland at Scone.

Macbeth is beginning to feel uneasy now that he is King. He is aware of the threat posed by Banquo and his son Fleance and arranges for them to be murdered.

Macbeth is spending more time alone. Lady Macbeth realises that she is no longer privy to her husband's confidences.

At a celebratory feast, Seyton reports back that Banquo is dead but that Fleance has escaped. Macbeth is shaken, but returns to his guests. Banquo's ghost appears only to Macbeth. Macbeth is horrified by its appearance. The guests, unable to see the ghost, are disturbed by Macbeth's unhinged behaviour. Lady Macbeth tries to calm the situation.

The guests leave, and Macbeth hints at more 'necessary' killings. Lady Macbeth is distraught.

1 Plot summaries

A lot has happened since **Part 1**. See how much you can remember.

a   Summarise the plot using between 45 and 50 words.

b   In small groups or as a class, take turns to retell the plot. Allow each person one sentence.

c   Write down five key words to sum up the main events.

d   Agree with a partner on the timescale of the action so far. Decide which scenes take place at night and which during the day. Consult your original playscript and make a chart of your findings. Compare your chart with that of another pair.

2 Read all about it

Macbeth is now King of Scotland. Your task is to make sure that all the people of Scotland are kept well informed. Design the front page of a newspaper to cover all of the latest events. Your lead story is likely to cover the crowning ceremony.

a   Try to include some other shorter stories, such as:

◆ The flight of Malcolm and Donalbain

◆ The strange noises heard on the night of Duncan's murder

◆ A political report looking into the implications of regicide

◆ A late update detailing Banquo's death

b   Decide on a selection of pictures.

c   Make the tone of your writing reflect your choice of tabloid or broadsheet style.

d   Plan the layout of your front page to have maximum impact on your readers.

14

3 Banquo

Banquo is a truthful and loyal character in sharp contrast to the false and disloyal Macbeth. He tries not to think about the witches' predictions concerning himself, and resists evil thoughts.

a Find the scenes in your playscript where Banquo appears. Speed-read these extracts to remind you of Banquo's thoughts and actions.

b Give examples of Banquo's behaviour to match the following words and phrases:

caring	honest
believes in God	brave
loyal	truthful
suspicious	

c Write a dying speech for Banquo. Think of all of the things he might have said if he had been able to.

d Write Banquo's obituary. What would he be remembered for? (He was a brave warrior; he left a son...)

4 The banquet

The banquet scene is often presented in lavish style. This contrasts with the evil world Macbeth now inhabits. Directors also have to decide how to present Banquo's ghost.

a In small groups act out this scene amongst yourselves. Use the original text or try to improvise a modern version.

◆ How does Macbeth speak his lines?

◆ How does he move?

◆ How do the other guests react?

◆ How does Lady Macbeth behave?

b Write an account of the banquet from the point of view of one of the servants.

5 Language in *Macbeth*

a Find quotations from your playscript to illustrate the following facts about Shakespeare's language in *Macbeth*:

◆ Some of the words used have now fallen out of use.

◆ Some of the words used have changed their meaning.

◆ Sometimes he wrote in verse.

◆ Sometimes he wrote in prose.

◆ His verse usually has ten syllables per line.

◆ Each of these lines usually has five beats or stresses.

◆ Sometimes the language is full of imagery.

◆ Sometimes it is very plain and direct.

ARMAMENTS

CAMOUFLAGE. ROYAL BARGE.

ROYAL STANDARD
PROW OF BARGE

BEAMS OVER

Order and disorder

The Elizabethans held strong religious views. They believed in an all-powerful God, and believed that all things had a purpose in the ladder of life. At the top of the ladder God was answerable only to Himself. They feared that a breakdown of this strict order would result in chaos.

b Find quotations in the playscript that show the breakdown of the natural order of life.

Darkness and light

Much of *Macbeth* is concerned with the dark side of human nature and the spread of evil. Shakespeare reinforces the darkness of the events by creating descriptions where darkness struggles with light.

c Find some examples of this type of imagery. Share your ideas with a partner or the rest of the class to produce a detailed picture of how well this technique is used in *Macbeth*.

d Using your playscript find some examples of Shakespeare's imagery that you find effective and some that you find less effective. Share your examples with a partner. Try to support your opinions by explaining the images.

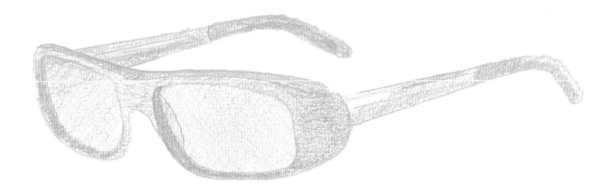

6 Quotations

In groups of four, look at the quotations on page 4 and find the ones from **Part 3**. Choose one to write out and illustrate for display.

7 Points to ponder

Write or discuss:

- Why does Shakespeare not include a coronation scene for Macbeth?

- What reasons does Macbeth have for hiding his plan to kill Banquo from Lady Macbeth?

- What is the implication of Fleance's escape?

- Why is it Banquo's ghost rather than Duncan's that comes back to haunt Macbeth?

- What does this Part show the audience about Macbeth's and Lady Macbeth's states of mind?

Macbeth: Part 4

Synopsis

Lennox examines the recent deaths of Duncan, Banquo and the bodyguards. He hints at Macbeth's guilt.

The witches complete their hellish brew as they wait for Macbeth. He demands that they summon up those who can answer his questions about the future. The apparitions tell him three things: to beware Macduff; that he cannot be killed by any man born naturally of a woman; and that he is safe until Birnam Wood moves towards his castle at Dunsinane. These initial warnings are dismissed, but Macbeth is disturbed by the sight of a 'bloody' Banquo and his heirs. He wakes up, screaming in his bed, to the news that Macduff has fled to England. Macbeth vows to kill Macduff's family and servants.

Ross tries to warn Lady Macduff. She is contemptuous of her husband's actions. Macbeth's hired hands arrive and murder her and her children.

In England, Malcolm tests Macduff's loyalty. Ross arrives with news of the slaughter. Urged on by Malcolm, Macduff vows to take revenge.

1 Lennox, Ross and Macduff

Under a dictatorship it is rarely safe for you to voice your thoughts openly. The characters in *Macbeth* have to use language carefully.

a Choose one of the above characters. Write five sentences to describe their characteristics and their role in the play. Compare your findings with another student.

b As a class decide which character is most important to the play, and which is least important.

c Look at how these characters are costumed. What effect does costume have?

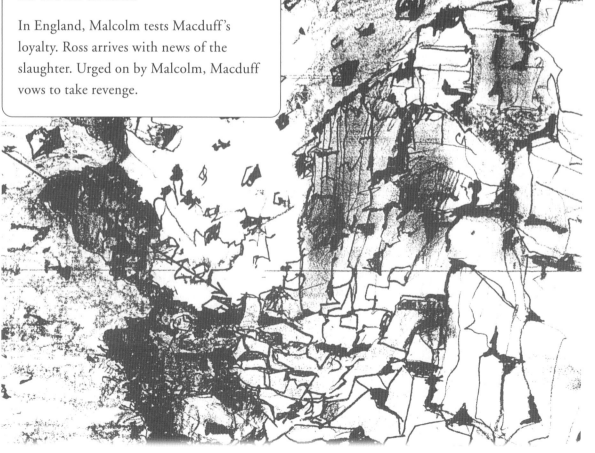

② The spell Act IV Scene 1

Macbeth has become obsessed by the desire
to know the future, and he demands answers
from the witches. He is now oblivious to the
consequences of his actions. Find this particular
place in your playscripts.

a Compare the original playscript with
the opening of **Part 4**. Discuss with a partner
where the cuts in this extract have been made.
What dramatic effect has this created?

b One of the best ways of understanding
the atmosphere of this scene is to act out parts
of it for yourselves. Use the extracts printed on
this page to experiment with staging the words.

◆ Try several people speaking together.
Whisper, chant, shout...

◆ Use sound effects or compose some music.

◆ Echo words to add emphasis.

Act IV Scene 1 Lines 4 – 38

Witches
Round about the cauldron go;
In the poisoned entrails throw.
Toad, that under cold stone
Days and nights has thirty-one
Swelter'd venom sleeping got,
Boil thou first i' the charmed pot.
Double, double toil and trouble;
Fire burn and cauldron bubble.
Fillet of a fenny snake,
In the cauldron boil and bake;
Eye of newt and toe of frog,
Wool of bat and tongue of dog,
Adder's fork and blind-worm's sting,
Lizard's leg and owlet's wing,
For a charm of powerful trouble,
Like a hell-broth boil and bubble.
Double, double toil and trouble;
Fire burn and cauldron bubble.
Scale of dragon, tooth of wolf,
Witches' mummy, maw and gulf
Of the ravin'd salt-sea shark,
Root of hemlock digg'd i' the dark,
Liver of blaspheming Jew,
Gall of goat, and slips of yew
Sliver'd in the moon's eclipse,
Nose of Turk and Tartar's lips,
Finger of birth-strangled babe
Ditch-deliver'd by a drab,
Make the gruel thick and slab:
Add thereto a tiger's chaudron,
For the ingredients of our cauldron.
Double, double toil and trouble;
Fire burn and cauldron bubble.
Cool it with a baboon's blood,
Then the charm is firm and good.

c Create your own recipe for 'Hell-broth'.

Act IV Scene 1 Lines 50 – 61

Macbeth
I conjure you, by that which you profess,
Howe'er you come to know it, answer me:
Though you untie the winds and let them fight
Against the churches; though the yesty waves
Confound and swallow navigation up;
Though bladed corn be lodged and trees
* blown down;*
Though castles topple on their warders'
* heads;*
Though palaces and pyramids do slope
Their heads to their foundations; though the
* treasure*
Of nature's germens tumble all together,
Even till destruction sicken; answer me
To what I ask you.

Witches
Speak.
Demand.
We'll answer.

3 Public and private

Macbeth is a play of great opposites. This is partly because true thoughts and feelings are concealed.

a Use the chart below to help you analyse how the characters and events reflect these opposites. You can put more than one character or event into each box.

loyal		disloyal
safe	**Macbeth's castle**	dangerous
good		evil
light		dark
natural		unnatural
public		private
order		disorder
brave		cowardly

4 Scotland and England

Scotland is now ruled by a tyrant. The news that is reported in Scotland will have to please Macbeth. In England the truth may be reported.

a With a partner discuss how the events of the play so far would have been reported in Scotland and England.

b Prepare scripts for television news bulletins to cover each of the Parts so far.

c Present your contrasting reports to the rest of the class.

5 Tour of Macbeth's country

a Design a leaflet advertising weekends away touring 'Macbeth's Scotland'.

Include a list of interesting locations such as:

Macbeth's castle
Scone
Dunsinane
Witches' cavern
Birnam Wood

Make your leaflet look and sound as tempting as possible. You could include menus, castle plans, guided walks through Birnam Wood, and so on.

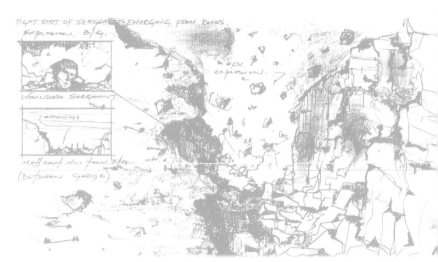

6 Quotations

In groups of three or four, choose three quotations on page 4 from **Part 4**. Prepare a freeze-frame for each one in turn. Present them to the rest of the class, who must guess which one is being shown.

7 Points to ponder

Write or discuss:

◆ What are the qualities of a good leader?

◆ What reasons does Malcolm have to be suspicious of Macduff?

◆ What has become of Donalbain since he fled Scotland?

◆ What are Macduff's thoughts and feelings at the end of this Part?

◆ What are the audience's feelings towards Macbeth at this point in the play?

Macbeth: Part 5

Synopsis

Lady Macbeth is sleep-walking, watched by a doctor and her lady-in-waiting. Lady Macbeth is trying to wash imagined blood from her hands. The doctor and servant are nervous of what they hear.

Meanwhile rebel forces assemble and prepare to join Malcolm's English army.

At Dunsinane Macbeth has received reports of the forces gathering against him, and he is becoming more desperate. He puts his trust in the apparitions' predictions. He vows that he will fight to the death.

Malcolm orders the troops to cut branches from the trees to disguise their numbers.

Macbeth is told of his wife's death. He thinks for a while on the futility of life. A messenger arrives with the news that the trees appear to be moving. One of the predictions is coming true.

Macbeth boasts that no naturally born man can kill him. Macduff reveals that his was not a normal birth. Macbeth accepts his fate and dies fighting. Malcolm, having led the English into Scotland, confers upon each of his Thanes the title of Earl.

1 Doctor's report

a Write a doctor's report about the mental state and behaviour of Lady Macbeth. Make the report an official document to present to Macbeth.

◆ What do her actions show?

◆ What do her words reveal?

◆ Who is looking after her?

◆ What cure could you suggest?

◆ As her doctor, what are you afraid she might do?

◆ Dare you suggest reasons for her actions?

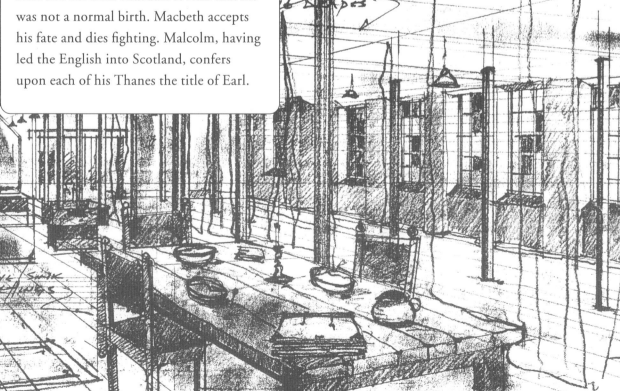

© 1998 Channel Four Learning Limited

② Out damned spot!

Box A contains Lady Macbeth's speeches from Act V Scene 1. The punctuation and capital letters have been removed.

a Copy out the speeches into Box B, putting back the punctuation and capital letters to create proper sentences and maximum impact.

Clue: The original speech is in prose. *Note:* the doctors' and servants' interruptions have not been included.

Box A

yet heres a spot out damned spot out i say one two why then tis time to dot hell is murky fie my lord fie a soldier and afeard what need we fear who knows it when none can call our power to account yet who would have thought the old man to have had so much blood in him the thane of fife had a wife where is she now what will these hands neer be clean no more o that my lord no more o that you mar all with this starting heres the smell of the blood still all the perfumes of arabia will not sweeten this little hand oh oh oh wash your hands put on your nightgown look not so pale i tell you yet again banquos buried he cannot come out ons grave to bed to bed theres knocking at the gate come come come come give me your hand whats done cannot be undone to bed to bed to bed

Box B

3 Tomorrow and tomorrow and tomorrow

> *Tomorrow, and tomorrow, and tomorrow,*
> *Creeps in this petty pace from day to day*
> *To the last syllable of recorded time,*
> *And all our yesterdays have lighted fools*
> *The way to dusty death. Out, out, brief candle!*
> *Life's but a walking shadow, a poor player*
> *That struts and frets his hour upon the stage*
> *And then is heard no more: it is a tale*
> *Told by an idiot, full of sound and fury,*
> *Signifying nothing.*

Act V Scene 5 Lines 19 – 28

a With a partner, read the above speech in a variety of ways:

whispering
confusedly
fearfully
sadly
angrily
reflectively

b Discuss with each other what you think Macbeth is saying about life.

4 Macbeth's final speech

It is unusual in a Shakespeare play for a character to die without a speech.

a Imagine what Macbeth might have said. Is he, for example, repentant? Write his final speech. Try to use iambic pentameter.

5 Themes

a *Themes* are important ideas that recur throughout the play. The words below show some of the important themes in *Macbeth*.

List them in order putting the most important first.

- ◆ Guilt
- ◆ Appearance and reality
- ◆ Bravery
- ◆ Evil
- ◆ Ambition
- ◆ The supernatural
- ◆ Order and disorder
- ◆ Individual conscience
- ◆ Divine justice
- ◆ What makes a man

©1998 Channel Four Learning Limited

6 Imagery

Imagery is the vivid use of language to create detailed pictures in the mind.

a Choose examples of phrases from the original playscript to illustrate the words below:

blood   darkness and light
disease   animals
sleep   hands
theatre and acting

7 Shakespeare meets Michael Bogdanov

The director of this particular version of *Macbeth* has chosen to make a number of changes to the original text.

a Imagine that he and Shakespeare meet to discuss the advantages and disadvantages of the decisions made by Bogdanov. Shakespeare is keen to uphold the original text and staging, while Bogdanov defends the cuts and raves about his updating of the staging. (Remember the music, motorbikes, guns, fire alarm, porridge-throwing child, and the dump truck which unloads Macbeth's body.)

b Write the dialogue that Shakespeare and Bogdanov have.

8 Macbeth: hero or villain?

Macbeth has been arrested and put on trial for his crimes.

a As his defence lawyer, it is down to you to make a case for his plea of 'not guilty'.

- He was well thought of, and considered a brave soldier.

- Who else could be blamed?

- Has he shown signs of remorse?

- Perhaps Lady Macbeth persuaded him with her taunts.

9 Quotations

Find the quotations from **Part 5** on page 4 and underline them.

Using the quotations for inspiration, design a poster advertising a forthcoming film or stage production of *Macbeth*.

10 Points to ponder

Write or discuss:

- What is the role of women in *Macbeth*?

- Would you like to be ruled by King Malcolm?

- What has become of Donalbain?

- Is *Macbeth* nothing more than a butcher?

- Is *Macbeth* a 'tale told by an idiot, full of sound and fury, signifying nothing'?

- Is ambition always destructive?

© 1998 Channel Four Learning Limited